GPS

GPS

Your Guide through
Personal Storms

DR. JAMES COYLE

iUniverse®

GPS
YOUR GUIDE THROUGH PERSONAL STORMS

iUniverse books may be ordered through booksellers or by contacting:

iUniverse
1663 Liberty Drive
Bloomington, IN 47403
www.iuniverse.com
1-800-Authors (1-800-288-4677)

ISBN: 978-1-5320-1441-3 (sc)
ISBN: 978-1-5320-1443-7 (hc)
ISBN: 978-1-5320-1442-0 (e)

Library of Congress Control Number: 2017902029

Printed in the USA

iUniverse rev. date: 03/27/2017

Contents

Preface

GPS: Your Guide through Personal Storms was conceived from my lifetime commitment to education and service in helping people navigate their personal rocky roads in life. After surviving a suicide attempt in 1977, I knew my life was spared for a mission. I was challenged with an assignment while working on my undergraduate degree in marketing. My professor had each student in the class write a personal mission statement. My first attempt was a six-sentence paragraph. The professor handed it back to me several times over the course of the semester until the mission statement was narrowed down to a short statement, one that changed the course and direction of my life: *helping people get to a better place.*

I received my bachelor's degree in marketing with a mission statement that guided and directed the passions of my heart and life. I opened a business in the service industry and became fascinated with the physical, spiritual, and emotional development of people.

I pursued educational opportunities to learn about physical development and became a certified personal trainer and fitness instructor, serving people in various ways in the health-and-wellness field.

I was ordained as a pastor in 1980 and began an incredible thirty-four-year journey of helping people find and define their spiritual paths through teaching, counseling, and community service.

I passionately pursued the emotional development of human behavior and earned my master's degree in counseling. A continued pursuit of my passion, coupled with my research and study, resulted in my earning a doctorate degree in counseling, with a focus on traumatic intervention.

In November 1980, I responded with the Clark County Fire

Department to the MGM Grand Hotel and Casino fire in Las Vegas. Eighty-seven people died, and 785 people were injured. At the time, I was a twenty-three-year-old chaplain, witnessing things that still haunt my memories. As horrific as that event was, it facilitated my preparation and navigation through the rest of my life's journey in helping and assisting people who experience traumatic events. I focused on the storms of life that people must weather for health and survival.

I concentrated my work in trauma centers, hospitals, and care facilities, providing support and care. I have worked beside fire departments and police departments for thirty-six years and have trained and led critical-incident support teams.

My professional counseling services have focused on helping children, marriages, families, and nonprofit and profit organizations work through the challenges of everyday life.

In 1996, I began a journey with the National Disaster Medical System (NDMS) that provided opportunities to deploy nationally and internationally. I have responded to fires, hurricanes, floods, tornadoes, earthquakes, and bombings. I am a founding member of the Department of Homeland Security and was honored as the Distinguished Member of the Year for the work in which I participated after the devastating earthquake in Haiti in January 2010.

Everything of which I have been a part or have studied has prepared me for what I am doing today. I currently am the human relations director for a funeral home in Cedar Rapids, Iowa, and assist people who are in their darkest hours, providing them with comfort care and guidance. Comfort care is being able to walk beside people who are having a difficult time navigating through life loss.

I teach college classes and assist local and statewide fire departments and police departments in responding to and training for critical events.

I am a keynote speaker in education and awareness for many topics that focus on developing health care and death care professionals. I also specialize in training and equipping first responders and caregivers with traumatic intervention in the work environment.

I finally have completed a book about my life's journey to help you, the reader, navigate through the storms of life.

Introduction

This book is about you and your personal GPS as you travel through the different seasons and storms of life. I will use personal stories, professional counseling, and a lifetime of educational studies and my background to give you wisdom in navigating the rocky roads of life.

We can't escape the stressors and the symptoms associated with stress in our lives, but we can learn how to manage them. *GPS* will provide direction, comfort, and care as you hold on to the steering wheel of life. The tools and insights I have gained from personal experience, education, and training will help keep you in your life's lane. *GPS* will use analogies to connect with, stories to relate to, and exercises to apply through your journey on the roads of life.

- We will uncover a guide to our thoughts as we explore the battleground of our thought lives that leads to choices that have different outcomes.
- We will learn to focus on the things that are most important to us, as these values become an anchor of our existence.
- We will look at a guide to navigating our days by giving it all we have, doing the right thing, and helping others.
- We will look at a guide to motivating our days by examining three of the most powerful words in our English language: hope, faith, and love.
- We will learn the significance of our experiences as we continue to move forward in life's journey.
- We will apply *GPS* principles to our new information.

When I was nineteen, I ended up in the deepest, darkest ditch of my life. My tires were flat, and mud was caked on the windshield. I thought the only way I could escape my pain and depression was to end my life. Divine intervention kept me from bleeding out.

I knew that my life was spared for a reason, but I didn't know why, nor did I know how to get out of my ditch. I began a soul-searching journey that led me to a life mission of helping people get to a better place. I became a youth pastor in 1980, which transitioned into senior pastoring for thirty-three years. My studies and education led me to counseling. I have been able to assist countless people with addictions and suicidal tendencies.

The pain of my own divorce allowed me to understand loneliness. I endured the struggle of single parenting, as I had full custody of my five-year-old and seven-year-old. I was blessed to get remarried to an incredible woman who had the same passion that ruled my life. She too has her doctorate in counseling. We share five kids and two grandkids and have lots of room for more. We have an incredible commitment to each other, our kids, and the families we serve.

My passion for helping people worked its way into traumatic intervention. I began a journey of assisting individuals and families in stressful circumstances. I have deployed all over the world and have helped thousands of people in their darkest hours. Both of my parents died in my arms, as I was allowed to take their last breaths with them. I have had the honor of being with hundreds of people as they transitioned out of their earthly body suits.

My life journey is to benefit you and your family in navigating through the storms of life. *GPS* has tools and exercises that I have used in my personal life, and in the lives of thousands of clients and friends, while living out my mission of *helping people get to a better place.*

CHAPTER ①

Guide to Navigating through the Storms of Life

In our journeys through life, we are always in one of three seasons on the road we travel. We are either driving *into* a storm,

driving *in* a storm,

or driving *out* of a storm.

The storm can last for minutes, hours, days, weeks, or even years; it just depends on the circumstances. The common thread to understanding all three seasons is to recognize that we are always surrounded by storms, no matter where we are driving. In the following pages, we will see how to navigate these storms of life by using tools that will assist us on our journeys.

I want to use an analogy to help you find your way through this book and through your life. Picture yourself as being your own personal vehicle. There are all kinds of elements outside your vehicle that will affect your drive. There are also all kinds of circumstances and events inside your vehicle that will affect your drive. *GPS* will help you identify the things you can control and the things you can't control. Understanding the things you can control will help you stay between the lines and out of the ditch. Being aware of the things you can't control will help guide you through the stressors of life that bring on anxiety, worry, tension, pressure, strain, trauma, and hassle.

All of our vehicles have a toolbox. The toolbox has tools that we have collected along the way, as well as room for more tools we will find in this book, and these will come in handy for different uses while navigating the storms that always surround us. Keep the tools close and available. I have spent a lifetime offering roadside assistance to

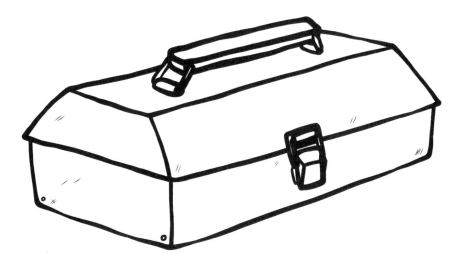

others while trying to tend to my own flat tires and car accidents. The GPS tools in this book have made a huge impact on my life and the lives of others who have traversed through storms.

In the first section of *GPS*, we will devote time and research to understanding the greatest battle we face: the constant war in our heads between what is right and what is wrong. It is a fight for both the known and unknown. These are the thoughts that consume us and hold us captive. We will explore a *GPS* guide to help us route and reroute our own thoughts.

The second section of *GPS* will look at keeping, adding, and sometimes removing the tools in our toolbox for our habitual and customary travels. We will also learn to use them while exploring the new terrain through the storms that are constant and never ending. These tools will assist us, when needed, through our day-to-day road trip.

The last section of *GPS* is devoted to finding and securing the things needed to keep us moving through our lives, no matter what season or storm we are in. A guide to motivating our days is essential to keeping gas in the tank, a foot on the accelerator, and a clear enough windshield to see where we are going.

I have a personal goal for you as you read, explore, and navigate the pages of this book. My heart's desire is to give you something to feel, something to remember, and something to do. My hope is to provide you with tools and information that can assist you, your family, your friends, and your associates through the difficult curves, potholes, steep climbs, and soft shoulders on the roads you travel.

CHAPTER 2

Guide to Controlling Our Thoughts

The biggest continual fight in our lives happens in our heads. The things we think about can consume us and hold us hostage, or they can set us free. The mind is the most powerful tool in our lives. The most difficult task we will ever face is learning how to control our thoughts, rather than allowing our thoughts to control us.

An old Native American legend talks of a powerful Chief who led his tribe and life with conviction and passion. One day, the chief's grandson sat on his lap and said, "When I grow up, I want to be a brave warrior and chief, just like you." The grandpa looked down at his grandson and said, "Son, there are two wolves in this life. There is a bad wolf, and there is a good wolf. The bad wolf will growl at you. He will chase you and pin you down. He will put you in a corner and not let you move. He will manipulate you and fill you with fear and guilt so you will be paralyzed, immobile, and imprisoned. Then there is a good wolf. He will walk beside you and protect you. He will guard you at night when you sleep. He will always be on the lookout for anything or anyone that is out to get you. He will be your companion and your strength." The grandson looked up at his grandpa and asked, "Which wolf wins?" The grandfather and brave chief said, "Whichever one you feed."

There is a constant battle for your thoughts, and it pits good against evil. In the spiritual context, it is God versus evil. The fight is on, and whichever wolf you feed will win.

Our thoughts and identities are like a jigsaw puzzle, as seen in the picture. Let's say we have ten major puzzle pieces that make up our

beings. Let's call them our core values (I'll identify them shortly). I want to walk beside you with an example of hearing the devastating, earth-shattering news that someone has taken his or her life. Suicide is so difficult to navigate because there are no answers to very difficult questions. Loved ones who are left behind commonly feel a sense of responsibility in being part of the decision to complete suicide.

I had the honor of walking beside and comfort-companioning a young lady who received the horrific news that her boyfriend had committed suicide after some unresolved conflict. Her world was shattered and broken, with the pieces of her existence scattered everywhere. The bad wolf was howling at her and cornering her with

thoughts of guilt, responsibility, and suicide. It becomes very difficult to not feed the bad wolf when its howling is all you hear. The puzzle pieces of her life that she thought were put together were now far apart; she felt she had no identity or reason to live. The devastation of her loss put a huge hole in her heart. She was fortunate to have a sister who represented the good wolf. Her sister had lost her fiancé a few years prior in an automobile accident. Both sisters were now experiencing the loss of a significant other at a young age. The two walked beside each other and learned ways to pick up the pieces. The puzzle picture with a hole in the heart represents an understanding that the emptiness of loss will never go away.

The pieces surrounding the emptiness are an attempt to build around the pain and loss. An awareness of the loss allows us to coexist with it, understanding that the hole will never go away.

The good wolf is the voice that can help put the pieces back together again after a traumatic loss. As we learn to feed the good wolf, we can begin to get our thoughts and identities back after a traumatic experience.

CHAPTER

What Controls Me?

Let's talk about how to gain control over our thoughts rather than having our thoughts control us. The diagram (figure 1) shows four circles. The innermost circle is our core values, the second circle is our attitudes, the third is our behaviors, and the fourth is our results. Outside the circles are external events and circumstances. Those are all the components of the storms of life. Some of the events and circumstances can be controlled, and some of them cannot. As you see in the diagram, there are arrows from the outside shooting in. Also in the diagram are arrows shooting from the inside out. When our thoughts are controlled by the bad wolf, the events and circumstances in our lives are the controlling factors (outside the circles). When our thoughts are controlled by the good wolf, our core values are the controlling agents for our lives (inside the circles).

Let's go through a couple of examples and look at the importance of understanding the battles we face for our thoughts. First, we'll examine the effects when our thoughts are controlled from the outside in (feeding the "bad wolf"). Let's say I am a freshman in college, and I receive an F in one of my core classes. This is the first F I have ever gotten, and it couldn't have come at a worse time. The F is the external event or circumstance. The *result*, in this instance, is the crushing news. The *behavior*, as a result of the news, is withdrawal. I feel defeated and deflated. I begin to search for and find excuses that validate the F. I hear and believe thoughts that school is not for me, and I begin to slack off in my studies, as other distractions begin to take priority. My *attitude* begins to shift, because now I don't care. My attitude toward school is tainted, and I can now justify my thought that school is a waste of time, and I don't need it anymore. I have no *core value* for school anymore.

What Controls Me

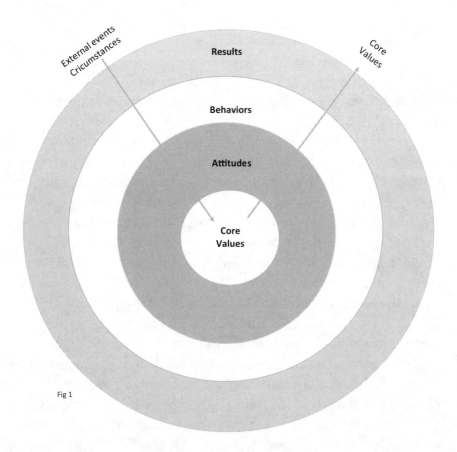

Fig 1

Now, let's look at controlling thoughts from the inside out (feeding the "good wolf"), using the same external event or circumstance of my getting my first F in college. My *core value* is that education is important and valuable. My *attitude* is rooted in my core value, so I look at this as a wake-up call to change direction before the direction changes me. My attitude toward school causes my *behaviors* to follow: I research ways to make up the grade and discover it means doing extra credit and new assignments. I talk to the professor and create a game plan to correct the wrong. The *result* is that the F actually drives me to dedicate myself more directly to my higher education.

Another example is the devastating loss of a loved one. A death is a horrible event with life-changing consequences, and it is an uncontrollable external event or circumstance. I will use my own experience of my dad dying in my arms. My dad was my hero, my best friend, my best man at my wedding, and one of my reasons for living. When I took my dad's last breath with him, a huge part of me died beside him. My insides were torn out of me as I wept and crawled into a fetal position, no longer wanting to live. Let's follow the outside-in cycle and feed the bad wolf. The *result* was the most difficult heart-wrenching thing I had ever faced. The *behaviors* were that I began to withdraw and isolate myself as a result of my pain and loss. Depression set in and ruled me. My work and relationships suffered. I was a snowball rolling down a mountain, headed for a collision. My *attitudes* shifted as I began to not care about the things I used to. My work and relationships no longer had the significance they once had, and I just did not care. I did not have a *core value* for living.

Eventually, I was able to start to slowly feed the "good wolf" and live from the inside out. One of the things my dad taught me was to learn from everything in life and utilize those lessons to make me stronger. I have a *core value* of learning and growing from the unfortunate happenings of life. Through this experience and core value, I was—and am—able to use the pain and loss of his physical being to help me. My *attitude* helped me honor that I was present to take his last breath with him. My *behaviors* allowed me to love and accept the things I do not have control of, while using these experiences to help others. The *results* are that I have been able to be with hundreds of people as they've taken their last breaths and assisted thousands of survivors in their storms. In a way, this book is a direct result of experiencing my father's death.

After a lifetime of studying human behavior, I firmly believe that our attitudes are rooted in our core values. All our behaviors are linked to our attitudes. The things we say and do (behaviors) are the results of an attitude. The results of our days and lives come from our behaviors, which are motivated by our attitudes, which are rooted in our core values. Thus, we essentially have four circles that are controlled and governed by two voices, a good wolf and a bad wolf. The events and circumstances are the same. The response and results follow the thoughts attached to the voice to which we are listening.

CHAPTER

What Are My Core Values?

Let's now talk about establishing our *core values*. Ideally, when the storms of life come, we want to be controlled by our core beliefs and *not* the event or circumstance.

I have a little challenge for you: I want you to write down ten of your core values. These are the things that you are most passionate about, the things you believe in, and the things that drive you. These core values could be faith, relationships, food, recreation, character, rest, and so on. Everyone has a different set of core values. As you write these down, rank them in order from one to ten. I encourage you to use the space on the following page to do this right now. Make a copy of your list, and post it on your refrigerator or place it next to your bed. You will find that the things that are closest to your heart are anchored in a core value.

Identifying your core values can lead to a defined picture of the kind of person you want to be and the kind of life you want to have. The problem is that we often have difficulty getting off the hamster wheel of our hectic lives to get in touch with our values.

Every core value is surrounded by seeds. The seeds are our thoughts, our emotions, and our actions. Our core beliefs about the world (is it safe or dangerous?), about other people (can we trust them or not?), and about ourselves (are we worthy or unworthy?) are formed early in our lives. Imagine a two-year-old who is hungry, alone, and crying. For each of the three following potential responses from the parent, the boy forms an accompanying belief about the world: (1) parent comforts, cuddles, and feeds the boy (*I am accepted and loved*); (2) parent ignores the child and lets him cry himself to sleep (*I am alone and abandoned*); or (3) parent chastises and abuses the boy and sends him to bed (*I am unlovable, and people are out to hurt me*).

Core Values

Deep seated beliefs, ethics, and morals

Write down your top 10 values and rank them

1)

2)

3)

4)

5)

6)

7)

8)

9)

10)

Core values will lead to a defined picture of the kind of person you want to be and the kind of life you want to have

My dad once told me the hardest eighteen inches in life is the distance between your head and your heart. In contemplating and researching your core values, think about connecting your head, your heart, and your hands. The connection between this "triple-H factor" (head, heart, and hands) is integrity. Integrity is when what you think, feel, say, and do are all on the same page. The connecting of your head with your heart leads to the skillfulness of the hands. One can't survive without the others. Without your mind and heart, your hands work aimlessly. Without your hands, your heart beats without action.

Let's learn some things about core values. They come from your character, integrity, and moral fiber. One beautiful option you have in life is to change your core values. Your attitudes, behaviors, and results will follow. To assist you in defining your values, explore your responses to the following:

- What am I thinking about?
- What am I feeling?
- What am I communicating?
- What am I choosing?
- What are my behaviors?

CHAPTER 5

Visualization Exercise

Now that you have identified your top ten core values, I want to walk you through a visualization exercise. Write each of your core values on a separate piece of paper and include the ranking you assigned (one through ten). You will have ten separate pieces of paper, each with one of your ranked core values. Then, wad them up into ten separate balls of paper. Mix the wads of paper over and over so that it is impossible to remember any order of your core values and place the pile in front of you. We'll use these papers to look at three specific and hypothetical storms of life:

1. Driving *into* a storm—you have just received news that you have cancer. The news has caught you off guard and has taken the wind out of your sails. As you are going into this storm, consider the fear of the unknown and your unpreparedness for what lies ahead. Randomly select two of your core values from the pile and place them in a separate pile without looking at them.

2. Driving *in* a storm—your house was in the path of an F5 tornado and was destroyed. All your personal property and lifelong mementoes are gone. You are left homeless. Randomly select two more core values and place them in the same separate pile away from your original pile. Keep them wadded up.

3. Driving *out* of a storm—you have lost the most significant person in your life. With this loss, you are drained, empty, and lifeless. You must figure out a way to gather yourself as you face the days, months, and years ahead. Randomly select three more core values and add them to the separate pile you've created.

You should now have three core values left in the original pile in front of you. Unwrap them. Examine what you have left, and see what's been taken from you. How do you feel right now? Do you feel violated? Do you feel angry? Do you feel abandoned? This is only a mental exercise of trying to understand the difficulty of navigating the highways of life, but the reality is that events and circumstances can rip your core values right out from under you, without your even being aware of it. Notice how you allowed the theft of your core values without any fight.

The bad wolf roams around like a predator, waiting and looking for any opportunity to steal your core values. His goal is to defeat you in the storms of your life. Your core values are the good wolf; they can keep you from sinking and straying. They help you survive the collisions of life. They allow you to think clearly and live life to its fullest potential.

Our cemeteries and prisons are full of people who can no longer find their core values; they have misplaced them, forgotten them, or have had them stolen from them without even knowing it. I have asked thousands of students and clients to identify the most important things in their lives, and it's amazing how many of them have never determined what those things are.

As we become more aware of how external events can influence our core values and shake our foundations, we can fight to hold on to the things that are truly important to us. Hold on to them, no matter how rough the storm is.

One of my core values is my wife. My *attitude* is that I worship the ground she walks on, and I adore her. My *behaviors* are directed toward making sure she is loved and cared for. The *result* is that I have an incredible marriage with an incredible woman. I have learned to hold on to this *core value* as we have traveled many years along the bumpy road of marriage. I am madly in love with my bride!

An essential guide to controlling our thoughts is knowing our core values and using them as an anchor. These core values are the things we hold on to through every season and storm. Do not let the events and circumstances of life steal your thoughts and values. Hold your thoughts and values captive to your core being and listen to the good wolf.

CHAPTER 6

Guide to Navigating Our Days

Lou Holtz is a former Notre Dame football coach. Always a great motivator, Coach Holtz gave dozens of inspiring talks to his players, trying to instill in them his beliefs about the basic principles of life. His speeches have motivated me in navigating my daily routine. Coach Holtz inspired me to live my life according to three rules: when I wake up, I'll (1) give it all I've got, (2) do the right thing, and (3) help someone. Let's talk about applying these three rules to our lives.

1. Give it all you've got. Growing up as an athlete and student, I was taught to give 110 percent or more. The reality of this statement makes no sense. We can only give what we have. The storms of life often empty our tanks. There is no way I can give 110 percent when my tank is empty. This first rule helps me understand that different minutes, hours, days, months, and years can fill me up or drain me. The book *How Full Is Your Bucket?* by Tom Rath and Donald O. Clifton, PhD, uses a simple metaphor to show how to *give it all you've got.* Rath and Clifton tell us that everyone has an invisible bucket. We are at our best when our buckets are overflowing. We are at our worst when our buckets are empty. The authors also tell us that everyone has an invisible dipper. In each interaction, we can use our dipper either to fill others' buckets or to dip from them. Whenever we choose to fill others' buckets with good words and actions, we in turn fill our own buckets with satisfaction and empathy.

The great physician Luke wrote, "Give away your life; you'll find life given back, but not merely given back—given back with bonus and blessing. Giving, not getting, is the way. Generosity begets generosity" (Luke 6:38 *The Message*).

So the principle here is to give whatever you have. If you are going into a storm and you have 80 percent to give, give it 80 percent. If you are in a storm and you only have 10 percent, give it 10 percent. If you are coming out of a storm and you have 50 percent, give it 50 percent. Give 100 percent of whatever you have when you wake up, and be totally honest with yourself. This will not only set the table for your day, but it also will let you off the hook for unmet expectations.

2. Do the right thing. In "35,000 Decisions: The Great Choices of Strategic Leaders," Dr. Joel Hoomans states that an adult makes about thirty-five thousand remotely conscious decisions each day. Dr. Hoomans gets even more specific, telling us, "This number may sound absurd, but the fact is, we make 226.7 decisions each day on just food alone."

Being responsible for making thirty-five thousand decisions each day can be overwhelming! Think about it. When we open our eyes, the choices begin. *I am going to open my eyes. I will turn off my alarm. I will use this foot to step out of bed. I will walk to the shower.* The power of our choices can make or break a moment, minute, day, year, and sometimes our entire lives. Each choice generally piggybacks on a previous choice. If I decide to wake up on the wrong side of the bed, this snowball begins collecting all the decisions that validate my initial choice. Eventually, this could result in my thinking, *I knew this was going to be a bad day when I woke up.* It is simple to say that the majority of our choices will dictate what follows. Our future is dependent on the present that was influenced by the past. And now the real question comes out: how can we possibly hammer through countless decisions and be assured that we are making the right choice?

Let's go back to the good wolf and the bad wolf competing for our attention. There is a constant war in our minds over doing the right thing. Our choices need to be rooted in our core values to keep us between the lines as we drive the roads of life. Thinking back to figure 1, remember to travel from the inside out. Our choices that are rooted in our core values steer our attitudes. Our actions and behaviors follow the paths of our attitudes. When my head rests on my pillow at night, I can review the results of the day and know where they came from.

There are so many choices in life that make you swerve outside the lines of your emotional, spiritual, and physical being. There are certain guidelines for you to follow that will keep you out of the ditch or from crossing the double yellow lines. If you want to know where you are going and if you are in the correct lane, look at your habits. Habits are formed from choosing the same action over and over again. Your habits determine your direction. The victory in staying in the correct lane and between the lines is to do the right thing day after day. If you can do that, you will protect yourself and your vehicle by staying accident-free.

Here are three guides to controlling your thoughts in a positive direction. First, *don't lose your character while you are trying to build your reputation.* Character is what defines you, while a reputation is what people think they know about you. Second, *don't sacrifice your family for your career.* You may win the admiration of those who don't matter while losing the love of those who do matter. Third, *don't sacrifice your personal core values for the values of the world.* Your core values will establish boundaries, while the values of the world will pull and push you away. These three guides will help you *do the right thing* and stay between the lines.

3. Help someone. If you can train yourself to have antennas up constantly and tune in to ways you can help others, your days will be far more fulfilling. Has someone ever said or done something for you that made you feel like a breath of fresh air in a polluted environment? A word, a phrase, or an act of kindness can help someone come out of a ditch. An act of kindness can lift someone above the circumstance. The apostle Paul addressed this in a letter to the church in Philippi: "Let each of you look not only to his own interests, but also to the interests of others" (Philippians 2:4 *The Message*).

The interests of others need to be our interests too. Certainly, we can look out for ourselves, but helping others (and filling their buckets) fills our bucket too. We must have open hands to give and receive.

There is a certain genius in generosity because what we let pass through our hands comes back to us. If we hold tight with clenched fists to what we have, nothing can be poured into our hands; they are already clinging tightly to something else.

While coaching a Little League baseball team, I witnessed a parent gripping the chain-link fence so tightly that his fingers and knuckles were white. His anger and resentment was the result of a decision I made not to let his son use a new bat he'd received for his birthday because the bat was far too big and heavy. The dad was physically and emotionally charged and wouldn't let go of the fence. I calmly reinforced the beauty of the birthday bat and the excitement of his son's holding it. I explained the danger of swinging something that could cause serious injury. I acknowledged his choice of equipment and helped him understand that the weight of the bat was the only point of concern. I watched the blood begin to flow back into his hands as he released his grip on both the fence and the situation. Sometimes the things we hold on to cause our circulation to stop flowing. Helping someone in the midst of a storm also helped resolve a conflict.

Several years ago, my family decided to perform random acts of kindness on a vacation that included a seventy-hour road trip. At every pit stop, we went into a convenience store and asked the cashier what his or her favorite drink was. One of the kids would find that drink in the store, and we would include it in our purchase. We'd then leave the drink on the counter and proceeded on our journey. The results were amazing for both the recipients and my family. Some cashiers ran out after us, some stood in shock with their jaws dropped, and some gave us the "What the heck?" stare. This project turned out to be one of the highlights of our trip. My kids learned how cool it was to give people something they liked. My wife and I were able to teach and model the practice of being kind to others without expecting anything in return. We all benefited from the simple and affordable act of kindness. Those favorite beverages—priceless.

CHAPTER 7

An Act of Kindness

I have a project for you. I use this project as part of a final exam for a college class I teach called Human Relations, and it was inspired by that road trip with my family. For the project you will take the following steps:

1. Choose an action or a behavior (act of kindness) that's out of the norm; the action or behavior must benefit someone else.
2. Commit to the act of kindness for a minimum of seven days.
3. Record the acts of kindness on the log sheet on the following page of this book. Examples of acts of kindness that are out of your normal behavior patterns include phone calls to loved ones who you have not had contact with, leaving affirmation notes for a loved one, volunteering at organizations that serve others, doing a daily act of kindness for neighbors, and so on.

In this project you will identify the chosen behavior, the recipient of the behavior, the effects the behavior had on the recipient, the effects the behavior had on you, and how this exercise will help make you a better person in the future.

Log Sheet: Acts of Kindness Project

Name of Recipient or Recipients: _____

Date	Start Time – End Time	Activity Details (what, when, where)

Total Time Spent (in minutes): _____

I've heard it takes around thirty consecutive days of doing something new to make it a habit. I have chosen to incorporate two things into every day of my life as habits. The first one is that I ask God for a divine appointment; to meet and be present with someone or something over which I have no control. The second one is that I look for an act of kindness that is intentional; something of which I am in control. Because I've committed to these two habits, my antennae are always up and ready to tune in to whatever opportunity presents itself. My days are filled with new territories and adventures as each day turns into an opportunity to *help someone* rather than an obligation. If we all choose to change obligations into opportunities, we will look forward to our days every time we wake up.

So far, we have talked about how to guide our thoughts and how to guide our days. If we can learn to control our thoughts and apply the three steps to our lives, our perception of life will change. Our perceptions of the world around us are what we base most of our thirty-five thousand choices on. The next part of our guide helps us determine how to motivate ourselves each day.

CHAPTER

Guide to Motivating My Day

Hope, Faith, Love

There is an interesting phenomenon on the volcanic island of Hawaii; you may have even seen it in person. In the most general terms, one side of the island is mostly lava. The majority of it is hardened and dark, though there are areas where hot lava flows slowly and freely down the mountain. It is barren and unnavigable for travel. There are boundaries that prohibit visitors. The other side of the island is paradise, with oceanfront properties, crystal-clear beaches, sacred pools with waterfalls, and tropical gardens that provide shade and nourishment. The same volcano has two sides to it, just as the choices of life do. On one hand, we can choose to feed the bad wolf. On the other, we can choose to feed the good wolf. Guiding our thoughts and navigating our days with the good wolf will help us reach paradise, rather than following the bad wolf down the path to hell. The following section is the critical part of moving our vehicles forward toward paradise during the storms of life.

We're going to turn our focus to a guide that will motivate us through our days. As we navigate our personal vehicles, I want you to think of each tire as having three spokes that equally separate the sphere of the tire.

The spokes represent the physical, spiritual, and emotional areas of our lives. When one of the spokes is missing or neglected, the performance of the tire is compromised. The result is that the ride is bumpy and can cause very serious alignment issues. We need to balance our tires (physically, emotionally, and spiritually) to make sure we have a smooth ride.

We will all have seasons when we get stuck in a ditch. Some are by choice, and some are not. These seasons can happen because of external events and circumstances that come out of nowhere and knock us off the road, or they can be a result of a few choices we made during the day. As a first responder, I have witnessed countless catastrophes that have included mass fatalities. As a counselor, I have talked with thousands of individuals who have experienced personal disasters. I have seen incalculable metaphorical personal vehicles blown, swept, and pushed into the ditches of life. There are times when we are going to need some assistance in realigning our tires.

Three words are the most motivating in the English language. These words are not tangible; they are words that embrace the mind, heart, and soul. Paul defines them in 1 Corinthians 13. They are *hope*, *faith*, and *love*. I have acronyms for these words as we break them down and absorb them into our minds, bodies, and souls.

Hope
Opens
People's
Eyes

Fear
Ain't
In
This
House

Living
Outside
Vulnerable
Experiences

Before we talk more specifically about each of these acronyms, I want you to picture yourself stuck in a ditch. Something has thrown you off the road, there's mud all over the windshield, and you can't accelerate out no matter how hard you try. Maybe you are imagining a specific storm that sent you off the road of life, or maybe you're keeping it more general. Now that you've visualized yourself in a ditch, let's talk about how to get out.

Hope

We'll start with the first powerful word in motivating our day, *hope—hope opens people's eyes*. Hope allows us to see beyond our current situations. It allows us to rise above the event or circumstance as if we are in a hot air balloon, looking down. Hope scrapes the mud off our windshields so we can see out and ahead. The windshield is much bigger than the rearview mirror—and for good reason. The rearview mirror reflects where we have been, while the windshield shows where we are going. Think about this in terms of our lives.

Too often we focus on what is behind us rather than what is ahead. And if our eyes are focused on the rearview mirror, we are in danger of staying in the ditch. If we do get out but keep looking back, we set ourselves up for another crash. We don't want to ignore the cause of the crash. We need to use the things behind us to guide our future journeys. One of the keys to victory in life is to use what is behind us to focus on what is ahead of us. We can't move forward if our eyes are focused on the past. We must look straight ahead through the bigger windshield. Second Corinthians 4:18 reads, "So we don't look at the troubles we can see now; rather, we fix our gaze on things that cannot be seen. For the things we see now will soon be gone, but the things we cannot see will last forever."

In my life, I have hope about many things, some are less serious, and some are far more significant. As an avid athlete and sports fan, I consider myself an equal-opportunity athletic enthusiast. However, football is by far my favorite. After the end of a long season, only two teams make it to the Super Bowl. Rather than focusing on the fact that my team usually doesn't make it, I choose to be hopeful that the next season will lead to the Super Bowl. This is an ongoing pursuit through the bigger windshield as I look forward to August every year.

On a much deeper level, there are many more serious events in my life where hope has carried the people I love the most through the hardest phases of life. I am going to take you back to the last conversation I had with my dad before he died in my arms. He fought a long, two-year battle with cancer and entered into a coma a few hours before his passing. On that last day, I watched and felt his body grow cold from his feet to his head, with the last remaining warmth above his heart. I was standing behind him with his head in my arms. In his last moment, his eyes popped open, and he stared up at the ceiling, as if he were looking beyond it. I asked him if he saw heaven. He said in a loud voice, "Yes!" I asked him if he saw angels. He said in a louder voice, "*Yes!*" I asked him if he saw Jesus. He said in an even louder voice, "*Yes!*" I then asked him if Jesus was coming to get him, and he said in his last fading word, "Yes-s-s-s!" He died at that moment.

What my dad lived for was his hope for a future beyond his earthly presence. What he showed me was the reality of his vision. I cannot thank my dad enough for this. He taught me to look out the big windshield and not be stuck on the rearview mirror. Hope allows me to focus on things I can't yet see through the windshield and to have confidence that there is a paradise waiting for me ahead.

Faith

The second motivating word to remember in our minds, bodies, and souls is *faith—fear ain't in this house.*

In an Internet article written by Sean Glaze, he recounts the story of the Trans-Alaskan oil pipeline, which began construction in 1975. When the pipeline was being built, many Texans went to Alaska to work. The Texans could only work a few hours in the freezing weather, yet the Eskimos could work indefinitely in the cold. A physiological study showed no difference in skin thickness, blood, or any other physical thing that would "explain the differences in the ability to withstand the temperatures." According to Glaze, "The answer came when they did a psychological study." The difference was that the Eskimo focused on the job that had to be done, while the Texan focused on the terrible weather.

You and I will focus daily on one of two things. We will either focus on how bad things are, or we will focus on the good that's around the corner. I want you to think of each side of your personal island as a separate enclosure. The first one holds you prisoner to the bad wolf and the darker, barren side of life. The second side holds you captive to the good wolf and paradise. One keeps you locked up in your fears and failures, and the other keeps you locked up in your faith and future. On my island, I want to be in captivity and protected by my faith and future, rather than unprotected in my fears and failures.

Our fears (*false expectations appearing real*) are a major exit into a ditch. If you incorporate *faith* into your core values and focus on eliminating fear from your house, fearful thoughts can be derailed. *Stop being afraid.* Instead of thinking about what could go wrong, think about what could go right. Become a devotee of what lies ahead, rather than a hostage to what lay behind.

The Latin word *movere* means "to move" and is the root of the word *motivation*. Faith motivates us and moves us toward our future goals. Think of faith as the accelerator in our vehicles. Faith is the ability to press the gas pedal toward the hope that we see through the windshield as we leave the ditches full of fears and failures behind.

Faith gives us the ability to accelerate toward the things we hope for through our windshields. I love the definition presented in Hebrews 11:1. "What is faith? It is the confident assurance that something we want is going to happen. It is the certainty that what we hope for is waiting for us, even though we cannot see it up ahead."

One of my journeys took me to the devastating earthquake in Haiti in 2010 when I deployed with the National Disaster Medical System (NDMS) on an International Medical Surgical Team (IMSURT). We were at the epicenter of the earthquake in Port-au-Prince, where more than 250,000 people died. The resulting wounds of the survivors were horrendous, and we performed countless amputations. While there, I met two people who changed my life. The first person was an incredible woman with tremendous faith. She'd had both legs and one of her arms amputated. In the core of her loss and pain, she smiled from ear to ear and was appreciative of our services. She couldn't speak English, but her faith spoke for her. Somehow, in the midst of a very dark storm that took the lives of her kids and loved ones, she still looked out the windshield and pressed on the accelerator to move forward. The ripple effect of her faith gave our entire team the motivation to continue our grueling and difficult work. The second person was a pastor of a small community church. His son had dengue fever and was being treated.

He came every day to pray with his son and bring encouragement to all the others. His infectious spirit brought hope and faith to the worst event and most horrendous circumstances his community and country had ever faced. He would bring his piano and set it up in the center of our base.

His music and worship resonated throughout the different tents that housed many of his people. He was an incredible presence not only to his fellow countrymen but to all of us who were assisting with limited resources. We were all overwhelmed, and these two beacons of light illuminated something positive in a negative environment.

In our own lives, every step we take creates a ripple. What we choose to do affects others around us, and if we choose to take those steps in hope and faith, we can have a hugely positive effect on our loved ones and anyone else touched by the ripple.

Throughout the last three decades, I've helped thousands transition from this life into eternal rest, both in person and by officiating funerals. I have noticed a huge difference between those who built their residence in faith, protected by the good wolf, and those who built their residence in fear, enforced by the bad wolf. Though I believe in God, this difference is not about any particular religion or belief. It is about choosing to live life in a way that feeds the good wolf and that focuses on hope and faith.

Love

The third motivating word to guide us in our minds, bodies, and souls is love—*living outside vulnerable experiences.*

The vulnerable experiences I'm referring to are the things we hear and face every day from the bad wolf. These are the potholes, soft shoulders, black ice, sleet, boulders, and obstructions that we navigate daily on the road of our personal journeys. These vulnerabilities can represent addictive behaviors, unforeseen tragedies, death, accidents, divorce, broken relationships, fear, abandonment, anxieties, disorders, and depression. The list of things that can trap us and keep us on the dark side of the volcano goes on and on. Living outside of and despite these events can route us toward paradise on the other side.

Let me paint a big picture and explain it through personal experiences. In Christianity, it is believed that God sent His Son to build a bridge into heaven. Jesus came and lived outside of sin to teach us and pave the way. Through His birth, death, and resurrection, we have access to heaven's gateway. The life of Jesus was rooted in love— living outside vulnerable experiences. Other faiths teach the same principles of overcoming the challenges of life and living through love.

I want to go back to my greatest mentor, my dad. During the last stages of his life, I would spend at least two hours every day playing cards with him and listening to him. Each day, I drove to his house, and if I was late, he would be standing on the sidewalk with his walker and oxygen tank, pointing at his watch as I pulled into the driveway. His infamous words still ring loudly in my ears. "You're late!" he'd say. "Get your ass in there." We played gin rummy, and he always won. We kept totals and tallied each game, and as he was entering into his final days, I took advantage of him and won enough hands to catch up. After I tied the score, I wouldn't play anymore. The final count was 9,879 to 9,879. Even though he was dying of cancer and understood that his time left on earth was short, my dad lived vulnerably. His choice to do so gave me hope and faith that was ruled and motivated by his love.

Out of all three of these words, the greatest is *love*. It is love that fills our tanks to drive out of the ditches of life. We can't move forward without it. Hope is essential to clear the mud off the windshield and pressing the accelerator, and accessing our faith is the only way to move forward. But if the tank is empty and there is no fuel, we can stare out the window and pump and pump the accelerator, but nothing will happen. We are not going to get out unless we have love to fill our tanks.

Love is what motivated my dad and so many others in their journeys. Have you ever been around someone who has so much love that it seems like he or she is not living in reality? It almost doesn't matter what the person is going through; he or she still radiates love, despite the awful things that life has thrown at him or her. Love is the real motivator to help get through the toughest circumstances.

I witnessed the most authentic power of love while walking beside a family whose fourteen-year-old son was on life support. They stayed and slept beside him for four days while his body was being tested and studied by a local donor network. In this young man's passing, his heart went to a ten-year-old, his lungs went to a sixty-nine-year-old, his liver and kidney went to a twenty-seven-year-old, and his other kidney went to a twenty-nine-year-old. Death is a vulnerable experience, and this family was able to live outside it. They watched and participated in knowing several lives were being saved by their son's vital organs. Their authentic love allowed life to continue in the darkest hour.

I know an incredible mom who lost two kids and a husband in a very short period. Her daughter lost her life in a horrible ATV accident. Her son lost his life to a brutal and senseless murder when he was shot in a parking lot. Her husband lost his life to a battle with cancer. At the trial of the murderer of her son, I was able to witness pure love shining through her darkest moment. She went up to the convicted felon and his family and said, "I forgive you." The only thing that can motivate authentic forgiveness is love.

I once held the hand of a woman as she died; she'd suffered from a flesh-eating disease. In that moment, she looked me in my eyes and comforted *me*. Her love washed over me and gave me strength to stay with her as she said her good-bye with love. The only thing that can motivate authentic transition is love.

I have stayed beside people as they detoxed from addictions, as their bodies suffered the symptoms of withdrawal. This is an opportunity to provide comfort care for them as they struggle to change their lives and begin their recoveries. The only thing that can motive authentic lifestyle change is love.

I have had the honor of assisting hundreds of people who were stuck in a ditch by extending a tow rope or a windshield scraper. Divorce, separation, loss of employment, loss of property, loss of investments and so many other losses are vulnerable experiences. The only thing that allows me to assist them is unconditional love, as my own personal journey has taught (and is still teaching) me to live outside my vulnerable events and circumstances.

The amazing thing about loving other people authentically and unconditionally is that it allows us to receive love in return.

So let's recap the three most powerful motivating words to add to our day.

- *Hope* (Hope Opens People's Eyes) allows us to see things beyond our circumstances.
- *Faith* (Fear Ain't In This House) enables us to move toward the things we hope for.
- *Love* (Living Outside Vulnerable Experiences) fuels us to live fully and authentically, despite tough situations.

Hope is the tool that scrapes the mud off the windshield so we can see something that is beyond our circumstance. Faith is the gas pedal that we press to get out and beyond the parked position in our ditch. Love is the fuel in the tank that is the source of our movement; without fuel, we can't go anywhere. It takes love for us to have enough faith to move beyond our circumstances. In our journeys through life, we are always either driving *into* a storm, driving *in* a storm, or driving *out* of a storm. The common thread to understanding all three seasons is that we are always surrounded by storms. Love is the fuel, faith is the accelerator, and hope is a windshield that's clear enough to provide direction.

CHAPTER 9

Understanding the Importance of Mile Markers

In ancient times, mile markers or milestones were used to measure the distance between certain points of travel. They came in all different shapes and sizes and were usually separated by a specified distance and identified by numbers.

In the United States we have a mile-marker system along the sides of our roads. The mile markers have numbers on them and can assist us in our travels. They help identify where we are, where we are going, and where we have come from. They also provide critical information to first responders in determining the location of accidents, along with coordinates for those in need of roadside assistance.

Mile markers are useful tools to guide us while driving into, in, and out of the storms that surround us. Establishing our personal markers will take a concentrated effort in identifying important events, circumstances, and the assistance we have received and encountered on the roads of life. Whether traveling daily, weekly, or yearly, these markers will help us in navigating old roads and new roads. Everything that has happened to us has gotten us to where we are so that we can prepare for where we are going. These markers will remind of us our past so we can be present for our future.

We all have personal stories that warrant the use of mile markers. I will share a couple of examples to show the importance of these guideposts. In 2006, the Midwest experienced devastating floodwaters that wiped out city after city, one of which was Cedar Rapids, Iowa.

We knew the rivers were rising, and I could feel that we were driving into a storm.

My community had a few days to prepare for what was coming. With my background in disaster deployments, I was able to assist in organizing volunteers. What took place over the next few weeks was an exhausting attempt to save lives and property.

When the flood waters arrived, my church was one of the buildings that was submerged in twelve feet of water. Though I'd responded with disaster relief teams to natural catastrophes all over the world for almost twenty years, I'd never actually been the victim of one. As soon as I was able to take off the hat of a first responder, I put on the hat of a disaster survivor. The neighborhood where our church was located comprised six blocks of 535 homes. Every home was buried under floodwater that was contaminated with sewage backup.

In my small neighborhood, every one of us lost physical, emotional, and spiritual possessions. The impact was devastating. People were homeless and desperate. The next several days were filled with anxiety, frustration, and hopelessness. The many years of experience and mile markers I accumulated along the way helped me cope with the conditions of this prolific event. These mile markers became guide posts for assisting myself and for assisting others during this storm.

Driving out of this storm was extremely difficult. We were a city in despair. For the first time, I also experienced personally what I had seen thousands endure in their personal storms as the result of a disaster. It was two years of legal paperwork, frustration, and unmet expectations. This event allowed me to create milestones in my journey as a first responder and a survivor. I now know firsthand what it means to lose everything for which you have worked so hard.

Twenty-six years ago, I went through a very difficult divorce. The pain of failure in something I believed in really set me back emotionally. As I headed into the storm, I had no problem establishing mile markers that validated the justification for ending my marriage. My mile markers were strong, and I built a very solid case. During this storm, however, I realized the ripple effect this decision had on my two incredible kids. The storm of divorce darkened my days, weeks, and hope for a future. Not only was I trying to find my identity, but I was trying to parent my two precious gifts of life as a single father. When I came out of the storm, I knew I wanted to use the mile markers I'd set before my divorce, during my divorce, and after my divorce to guide me in future relationships. Through the grace of God and His guidance, I was able to realign my wreckage onto the most beautiful road of marriage. The mile markers have proven to be critical guideposts in staying on the road I travel with my incredible bride, and they continue to lead me in the right direction. I love her more today than yesterday as a result of understanding the power of mile markers in the past, in the present, and in the future. It took several years to understand the power of these road signs. They are aids in designing new roads and repaving torn and worn roads.

Many of the roads we travel have already been traveled, both by us and others. These are the same roads that get us back and forth every day. I encourage you to set up your mile markers daily, and use the previous ones to keep you between the lines.

Conclusion
Applying Your GPS

The greatest reward from our road trip is not what
we get out of it but what we become through it.

In this book, we have used the analogy of driving our personal vehicles on the roads of life using the GPS (Guide through Personal Storms). We've talked about the importance of controlling and steering our thoughts. There is a constant battle competing for the thirty-five thousand choices we make each day. Our thoughts are often influenced by listening to the good wolf or the bad wolf.

We spent time recognizing events and circumstances that occur throughout our lifetimes. Some of these we can control, but many of them we cannot control. Whether we can or can't control situations, we learned how important it is to hold on to and anchor into the things that are most important to us—our core values.

Defining and understanding our core values helps keep us centered in establishing our attitudes. From our attitudes come our behaviors. Our behaviors then lead to the results of our days, months, and years. Being controlled from the inside out is focusing on our beliefs and passions. Being controlled from the outside in is focusing on the events and circumstances. We are much better off when we are guided by our passions, beliefs, and values.

We established three daily rules with which to navigate our day. Each day that we wake up we can give it all we have, do the right thing, and help someone. If we use these three guides, we can turn our day into the most productive and fulfilling day, no matter if we are entering a storm, traveling through a storm, or coming out of a storm.

We defined three of the most powerful words in our language: hope, faith, and love. Hope is being able to see through the mud on our windshields. Faith is being able to press on the accelerator to get us moving toward the things we hope for. Love is the fuel that fills our tanks so we can accelerate toward the things we hope for. Without love, our tanks are empty.

We looked at establishing personal mile markers to help identify the important events, circumstances, and roadside assistance we encounter in our travels. Here we come to realize that everything that has happened to us is part of our journeys. These reminders of our past are guiding our present and paving the way for our future.

The whole purpose and intent of *GPS* is to give you something to feel, something to remember, and something to do on your unique road trip through life. If you can learn to control and manage your thought-life; stay true to your core values; live by the three rules of life; stay motivated by hope, faith, and love; and use your past experiences to guide you, you will find paradise on the opposite side of the volcano. The greatest reward from our road trip is not what we get out of it but what we become through it. Aloha!

GPS TOOLS 4 LIFE

My first experience with a Midwestern small-town parade was sweet. Riders on lawn mowers, tractors, wagons, buggies, and basically anything that had wheels on it traveled down a designated route, and the riders smiled, waved, and threw out candy. It was amazing to see how many spectators chased after a Jolly Rancher or Tootsie Rolls. Our personal vehicles can serve the same purpose in our own lives. We all have an opportunity to distribute sweet gifts along the way. The following are a few GPS *Tools 4 Life* to keep us safe and productive on the road.

Tools
4 Life

If You Want Change, Become It

I have found that the best way for me to make a difference is to *become* the difference. Whether parenting, coaching, pastoring, or counseling, the best action I can take to create action is to remain passionate and willing to become the end result. Here are some tools that might help in overcoming the potholes in making a difference.

Do something about it. Don't hesitate or wait around for someone else to step in to do something to make the situation different and better. Do it yourself, and do it quickly.

Spend the time needed for change. Never put off or give up on a goal that's important to you. Life is shorter than it sometimes seems. All we have is today, as tomorrow may not come. Follow your heart and passion now.

Always be a student. Experience, learn, and absorb all the knowledge you can. Prepare yourself for change by keeping your mind fresh with new opportunities to change. If you stay ready, you don't have to get ready.

Stop being afraid. Instead of thinking about what could go wrong, think about what could go right!

Tools
4 Life

Forgiveness Shakes Off the Dirt

"Shake It Off," on the United Christian Broadcasters website, recounted an old story about a farmer and his mule. According to the tale, the farmer's mule fell into a well. He had no way to get him out, so he decided to bury him there. He dumped a truckload of dirt on top of the mule. The mule started snorting and kicking until he worked his way to the top of the pile. Truckload after truckload of dirt was dumped into the well, and the mule kept shaking it off—until the dirt reached the top of the well and the mule walked away from it. What was intended to bury him ended up helping him to come out on top.

The point here is that no matter how bad it looks or feels, there will always be a way out, and the piles of dirt that were meant to bury you will eventually help you out of the situation. The key to coming out on top is to forgive the dirt and shake it off, or you will get buried. Forgiveness can't change the past, but it can change the future. Shake it off and walk away.

Tools
4 Life

Things Must Work *in* Me before They Work *for* Me

Have you ever tried to do something because it worked for other people and you wanted their results? There are thousands of diets designed to curb your appetite. Thousands of exercise routines are "guaranteed" to get you in shape. There are thousands of products to help you quit smoking, drinking, and other addictive habits. Billions of dollars are spent on products advertised on infomercials and commercials to get you to change into something new and different. *Breaking news: Things must first work* in *us before they work* for *us!* Change is not about joining a gym or club so you can be part of something. It is not about opening up your wallet to spend on a "miracle" product. It is about an *inward* change of your heart. When we believe, we chase with our hearts. The results working *in* us before they work *for* us. If we want results, we must meet the inward conditions of our hearts.

Tools
4 Life

Thankfulness Buries the Killer Cs

Have you ever noticed that some people seem to maintain an attitude of thankfulness and gratitude, regardless of what happens around them? They see the good in difficult people, they see the opportunity in a challenging situation, and they appreciate what they have, even in the face of loss. These people have the ability to bury the "killer Cs" that can overtake us and cripple us. The killer Cs are criticizing, complaining, and controlling. Here are some benefits of eliminating the killer Cs with thankfulness.

Thankfulness buries the critic that judges and finds fault. When we are grateful, our eyes and thoughts look up to someone, rather than looking down on someone.

Thankfulness buries the complainer who is never satisfied. When we are grateful, our focus is on appreciating what we have versus focusing on what we don't have.

Thankfulness buries the controller who has a tight hold on everything. When we are grateful, our grip on the steering wheel loosens, and amazing and unexpected things happen.

Difficult Traditions

Are you looking ahead at a mountain of traditions that are overwhelming and unbearable? Is it impossible to put on a game face when everyone around you is joyful? Has the pain of sorrow and loss blurred any vision of seeing ahead? So many things knock the wind out of us; death of a loved one, death of a pet, divorce, a looming relational end, diagnosis of life ending disease, financial hardship, etc...... Here is a very short list of 10 tools that can help you navigate the difficult weeks ahead.

- No is a complete sentence. Use it. Well-meaning people will try to fill your schedule.
- It's OK to take a year off. One thing for certain, next year will roll around quickly.
- Decide what you don't want or like and replace it with comfort.
- Have an exit strategy to get off the holiday hi-way.
- Tell people what you are comfortable with.
- Create your own personal traditions.
- Take on a holiday project that helps someone.
- Close your eyes and remember something that made you happy and smile back.

- Maybe something was left undone. Complete the project or deed in honor of your loss.
- Plan for something in January

Surround yourself with people you trust and add new tools to your toolbox of survival. You are loved!!

Tools
4 Life

Let it Grow

This is a great time of year if you like watching finals of sporting events. Whether it is the Triple Crown, NBA, NHL, MBA, NFL, and other sporting venues, there is always those who don't win. The recent Belmont Stakes race captured the hearts of many as we wanted so badly to see a Triple Crown winner. Here is the most important lesson in life; "All athletes are disciplined in their training. They do it to win a prize that will fade away, but we do it for an eternal prize. So I run with purpose in every step. I am not just shadowboxing. I discipline my body like an athlete, training it to do what it should." 1 Corinthians 9:25-27 Everything we go through in this life is to mature us and complete us for a greater work. The brother of Jesus captured some very encouraging words for all of us. "Dear brothers and sisters, when troubles come your way, consider it an opportunity for great joy. ³ For you know that when your faith is tested, your endurance has a chance to grow. ⁴ So let it grow, for when your endurance is fully developed, you will be perfect and complete, needing nothing." James 1:2-4 Let it grow!!!!

Tools
4 Life

Changing the "Why" to "How"

Life is a roller coaster of ups and downs. Every valley and every mountain top has a lesson, if I am teachable. I am accepting when it comes to my own difficulties. But when it is others' pain I tend to swim in the "WHY," which leads to anger, frustration, depression, anxieties, etc...... I lose sleep, weight, hair, desire, hope, passion, patience, perseverance, and purpose. I build a case against God and against others. Why them and not someone else? Why them and not me? So, for me to survive in someone else's pain along with my own I must switch to "How" rather than "Why." How can I love God more in this situation? I need to swim in the "How" to love Him more despite the horrible circumstances. Here are a few tools: 1) Accept *"Father, if you are willing, take this cup from me; yet not my will, but yours be done."* Luke 22:42 2) Be Free *"Out of my distress I called on the Lord; the Lord answered me and set me free."* Psalm 118:5 3) Be in Peace *"Do not let your hearts be troubled and do not be afraid."* John 14.27

Humility Optimism Energy

A **HOE** is an ancient and versatile agricultural tool. It is used to move small amounts of soil. Like the hoe, we too are used to stir up the ground around us for Kingdom work. Another use of the hoe is to agitate the ground for weed removal and control just like our role is to agitate the ground around us to remove the weeds of evil and control their existence. The hoe is also used for "hilling" which is piling soil around the base of a plant. We too are encouraged to build a foundation around the work of God as he grows and matures us and those around us. Another goal of the hoe is creating "drills" - narrow furrows and shallow trenches for planting. We have opportunities every day to plant seeds for the work and Glory of God. Three core values that we can implement into our being are; (1) **Humility** – *"Do nothing out of selfish ambition or vain conceit. Rather, in humility value others above yourselves, not looking to your own interests but each of you to the interests of the others." Philippians 4:3-4.... 2)* **Optimism** *- ²⁸ We know that God makes all things work together for the good of those who love Him and are chosen to be a part of His plan. Romans 8:28....***Energy** *- Forgetting what is behind and straining toward what is ahead, I press on toward the goal to win the prize for which God has called me heavenward in Christ Jesus. Philippians 3:13-14* "The difference between stumbling blocks and stepping stones is how you use them." – *Unknown*

Tools
4 Life

Life Socks

Socks cover one of the most vulnerable parts of the body. They are designed to provide an inner protection of the sole inside the shoe as the feet move in a direction. Picture a sock covering your heart as it protects the soul inside the body as your life moves in a direction. If my sock is wet and dirty, then my soul is wet and dirty. If my sock is clean and pure, then my soul is clean and pure. "Hatred stirs up trouble; love overlooks the wrongs that others do." Proverbs 10:12. Is your heart sock made of pain, hurt, anger, and unforgiveness? If it is you will have a life of conflict and unrest. Is your heart sock made of love? If it is you will have a life of peace that surpasses all understanding. *"4 Love is kind and patient, never jealous, boastful, proud, or 5 rude. Love isn't selfish or quick tempered. It doesn't keep a record of wrongs that others do. 6 Love rejoices in the truth, but not in evil. 7 Love is always supportive, loyal, hopeful, and trusting.8 Love never fails!"* 1 Corinthians 13:4-8

Tools
4 Life

Making It Real

Death Valley, the hottest place on the west coast, is a desert floor that provides false hope and life in the form of a mirage. The more intense the heat gets the more beautiful the mirage becomes. People today are chasing and putting their faith in false securities turning over every rock along the way to try to find the secret. Some seek it through money and success, others pursue it in pleasure and success, The Apostle John (1 John 1:1-7) unwraps 4 guidelines that provide hope and purpose in "Makin it Real" The first is to secure the right foundation, the Word of Life. The second is to surround yourself with the right companions, having fellowship with one another. The third is to have the right source, God is light and there is no darkness. And the fourth is to have the right goal, to walk in the Light as He is in the light. So here is the ground work for "Makin it Real": the right foundation, the right companions, the right source, and the right goal. How real is your life?

Tools
4 Life

Be an Olympian
TRAIN

As our family is glued to the Olympics rooting on the World's top athletes, I am inspired by their individual stories and commitment that prepares these athletes to do their best as they compete. But what is even more compelling than the highest ski jump, the elegant figure skating, the fastest bobsled, and the flare and flash of snowboarding is the Olympic spirit that runs in their veins. The timeless wisdom of the Bible offers 5 core values that these athletes **T R A I N** with. May we all incorporate these values into our personal lives as we continue to develop the Kingdom Olympic Warrior that we are called to be. The Olympics are full of teachable moments and the Bible is full of character training.

Triumph: Approach both success and failure gracefully
Respect: Treat others as you would have them treat you
Alliance: As iron sharpens iron, so a friend sharpens a friend.
Instinct: Drive for excellence
Never: Never, never, give up

Tools
4 Life

Beyond Your Boundaries

A four-year-old was out riding her brand-new tricycle. Mom had to go inside for a few minutes and had a stern conversation establishing the boundaries. She pointed to the neighbor's driveway on one side and a tree on their property for the other side. "You are to stay between the driveway and the tree. If you go past either you will get a spanking." She backed up her trike to mom's feet and said; "You might as well spank me now. I have places to go." We all have places to go beyond the boundaries of our youth. You are created for a unique purpose in this life and the only way to find out that purpose is to pedal beyond the safe zone. *²"Enlarge the place of your tent, stretch your tent curtains wide, do not hold back; lengthen your cords, strengthen your stakes. ³For you will spread out to the right and to the left. Isaiah 54:2-3* Keep pressing forward toward your God given identity. Take an inventory of the passions that drive you. Those are the passions that drove our little 4-year-old try-cyclist. Don't allow the speedbumps, tight curves, pot holes, and cracks in the sidewalk keep you from pedaling. Don't let the driveways and trees prevent you from being who you were created to be. On your mark, get set, GO!!!!

Doing the Right Thing

I just read a recent story that captured my heart. It involves a 19-year-old college basketball player who has inoperable brain cancer. The NCAA gave special permission for two colleges to begin play before the normal starting date. The results of "doing the right thing" filled an arena, a state, a nation, and a world that is in desperate need of hope and purpose. The cloud of an act of kindness rains and soaks those who are fortunate enough to be under it. This is an example of cross-pollinating with corporate America, the beaurocracy of higher educational institutions, the council of medical doctors, and the will and desire of a young, determined athlete. When we come together to do the right thing, barriers become bridges and bridges become a path to walk and live each day as it is meant to be. Doing the right thing gives us a *get off the hamster wheel jail free card.* This 19-year-old girl turned a death sentence into a live lesson. This live lesson is what we need to live each day, as it is our beginning not our end.

From the Root to the Fruit

There are over 23,000 types of trees...and every type has roots. The root system of a tree usually grows between two to four times the width of the tree, establishing a foundation for growth and fed by the water and minerals of the soil. The better the soil, the stronger the roots, the healthier the tree. You can't see the roots, but they determine the health of that tree. And so, it goes in our lives. We are fed by our unseen values and how we water them. If we have no values to water, then our lives will bear no fruit. If we have a beautiful piece of fruit in our life and we pull it from the source that is fed by its values, then the appearance begins to fade and the inside begins to rot. Bad soil or bad environment prevents our values to be rooted in good soil. You know people like this; don't be one of them. Root your life in good soil and water your values. In other words, ground yourself and surround yourself with strong core values. Water them and this will help you grow strong roots physically, emotionally, and spiritually. Once you identify and feed your core values don't fall from the tree. A bad apple doesn't fall far from the tree. Stay connected!!

Tools
4 Life

Self- Discipline from the Inside Out

Self- discipline is the fuel to keep us moving in a positive direction. A friend recently said "Say no for a short time so you can say yes for a lifetime". What a perfect defining statement of letting self-discipline guide our journey. Self-discipline must become a lifestyle. It is not a onetime event. It is a short time commitment that leads into a lifetime habit. If we can anchor our choices in our core values, the priority of our decisions will keep us focused on lifetime results rather than short term satisfactions. Part of the success of this is to reward yourself at the finish line verses along the way. We must learn to eat our vegetables before the dessert. We should not get a participation medal for trying. We should get the rewards for victorious wins at the time of jumping the hurdles in a lifelong race. Don't make excuses along the way. An excuse is an escape from responsibility. Stay focused on the results of the work rather than the difficulty of the work. Focus on the benefits of doing what is right. This is self-discipline from the inside out. Stay true to your core and keep moving in confidence toward your desired results.

Tools
4 Life

Turning a bad ending into a new beginning

Have you ever been lost between the past we know and future we don't know? There is so much pain and confusion in handling losses like; a parent, a child, a marriage, a job, a reputation, health, and finances. Grief is a natural reaction to loss. Buried grief is unfinished business that rears its head in depression, anxiety, PTSD, etc.... Completed grief allows us to remember the past that helps build the future. Allow grief to complete itself through different stages these are a few of many:

Shock - "This can't be happening"

Anger - "It's not fair, I don't deserve this"

Bargaining - "I'll do anything to change this"

Depression - "There's nothing worth living for"

Acceptance - "I have to try again"

Faith transforms every ending into a new beginning.

Unlock Your Mind

"All that we are is a result of what we have thought" Abraham Lincoln. We create our own world through our thoughts. Think about the clothes we are wearing, the chair we're sitting in, the house we sleep in. Before these objects took on their shape, they were a thought. Think of the computers we use and the phones we are attached to. They were all created through an idea and transformed into a product. Likewise, we create our own little world through the power of our thoughts. We are the writer, the director, and the star of our own life movie. One of my favorite scriptures is recorded in *Ephesians 12: 2 "Do not conform to the pattern of this world, but be transformed by the renewing of your mind."* One of the greatest accomplishments we can achieve is breaking away from the patterns of the world and becoming the person we are supposed to be. It is up to us to protect what comes into and what comes out of our mind. There is plenty of negativity that would like to take up residence in our mind. Guard your mind and your thoughts and only allow the positive to find a home.

Tools
4 Life

The Vision, The Venture, & The Victory

Have you ever set out to do something that you believed was the right thing to do and God had other plans? I know I have built my case and presented my plans before the Lord only to find God redirecting my path. Psalm 37:23 says *"The steps of good men are directed by the Lord. He delights in each step they take."* This has applied to me personally, my family, finances, moves, business, decisions, dating, church...... I also believe the "stops" of good men are ordered by the Lord. We must be sensitive to the Holy Spirit. It is vitally important for all of us to do things God's way and not our way personally and corporately. If we insist on having our way, God may do something that we won't like in the end.... He may let us do it our way. Been there, done that!! We should pray every day, "Lord, I am available today for you to tell me where to go, what to do, what to say, when to say it, and when to do it." The vision is to see ahead, the venture is to take the steps in moving forward, and the victory is knowing you are being used to make a difference.

Tools
4 Life

What's on the Other Side of the Sandbag?

Much of what we do day in and day out doesn't seem to matter until it becomes a paint stroke on the canvas of our life. We can go through life filling sandbag after sandbag with the mundane effort of shoveling dirt. There is nothing glamorous about a shovel and a pile of dirt that wears us out physically and emotionally. If we can turn our labor into an act of love our sandbags have new meaning. Every sandbag we fill becomes part of a dike which is much bigger than what I ever thought. What's on the other side of the sandbag are events and circumstances that can have devastating effects in our world. Mother Teresa wasn't motivated by fame or wealth. She was consumed with a passion to fill her sandbags with ministering to the unmet needs of the forgotten people in the slums of Calcutta. If we can embrace all our efforts into helping those around us, we can bring peace in chaos. We may never know what is on the other side of our sandbag. What we need to know is that we all have the opportunity to make a difference. One of Mother Teresa's slogans was; "A life not lived for others is a life not lived at all."

Tools
4 Life

Passion, Perseverance, Purpose

Have you ever finished something because you knew you had someone in the shadows rooting you on? Have you ever gotten strength from a crowd of people who have been there and done that? Have you ever been all alone and al l you have is what is in your gut? Have you ever felt deserted with nothing in the tank to keep you going? All of us will at some time be strengthened by the faith that others have in us. All of us at some time must face the lonely journey of having to gut-it-out. There is an eternal motivator that will keep your engine running on the coldest of nights. There is an eternal motivator that will move mountains. Jesus relied on it to get to the finish line and so must you and I . "Because of the joy awaiting Him he endured the cross." Hebrews 12:2 If we can fix our eyes on Jesus, He will pioneer and perfect our faith. The catch to this is; "The joy of the Lord is my strength." Nehemiah 8:10. His joy fuels my passion, perseverance, and purpose.

Tools
4 Life

Roadblocks in Relationships

How do you rate yourself in building relationships? Are people naturally drawn to you or is there debris on the road preventing access from both directions? Here are a few things that could prevent people from entering onto a common road with you. **Moodiness** – moods are like rollercoaster's that have highs and lows and wild turns. If people never know what to expect from you they will stop expecting anything. **Perfectionism** – unreal expectations are concrete barriers. People respect the desire for excellence but hit a wall when their chin can't meet the height of the bar. **Pessimism** – people don't like to be rained on by someone who sees storm clouds on a sunny day. **Arrogance** – nobody wants to be in a relationship with someone who thinks he/she is better than everyone else. **Insecurity** – If you are uncomfortable with yourself and who you are, others will be too.

Tools
4 Life

Small Still Voice

I was recently in downtown Chicago using my GPS, when the voice started spitting out different directions at every intersection. I spent an hour circling around tall buildings and congested store fronts, only to find myself right back where I started from. As I called the destination in a frustrated panic, the operator gently said, "Turn off your GPS. They don't work downtown. Now look to your right. We are the tall building you're staring at." I realized that the resource I had become so dependent on had let me down. In the center of giant obstacles, communication becomes scattered. When communication breaks down, fear and panic sneak up on us; we need to **STOP** and listen. *"Go out and stand before me on the mountain," the Lord told him. And as Elijah stood there the Lord passed by, and a mighty windstorm hit the mountain; it was such a terrible blast that the rocks were torn loose, but the Lord was not in the wind. After the wind, there was an earthquake, but the Lord was not in the earthquake. And after the earthquake, there was a fire, but the Lord was not in the fire. And after the fire, there was the sound of a gentle whisper. When Elijah heard it, he wrapped his face in his scarf and went out and stood at the entrance of the cave."* In the midst of our chaotic and hectic life, God's voice is there. Turn off the GPS and listen.

Tools
4 Life

Spread the LOVE not the Offense

One of the greatest tools of wisdom is recorded in Proverbs 17:9 "He who covers over an offense spreads love, but whoever spreads the matter separates close friends" One of Noah's sons found him in an embarrassing spot after a tough night. The son went out to spread the offense (gossip) when his 2 brothers shut him up and covered their dad's shame with an act of love. The consequence of spreading someone's mistake is never good. The immediate gratification can make me feel good or look better as I beat my chest and wave my flag. The reality is by repeating the matter I am distancing myself from my close friends. Once I learn to look at others as being more important than me I see them differently. Rather than looking down on someone I look up at them. Am I spreading love or am I spreading the offense?

**Tools
4 Life**

Stop, Listen, Absorb, & Act

Here are some wise words from an anonymous poet. "If you can start the day without caffeine: if you can get going without pep pills; if you can always be cheerful, ignoring the aches and pains; if you can resist complaining and boring people with your troubles; if you can eat the same food every day and be grateful for it; if you can understand when your loved ones are too busy to give you any time; if you can forgive a friends lack of consideration; if you can overlook it when those you love take it out on you, when, through no fault of your own, something goes wrong; if you can take criticism and blame without resentment; if you can ignore a friends limited education and never correct him; if you can resist treating a rich friend better than a poor friend; if you can face the world without lies and deceit; if you can conquer tension without medical; if you can relax without liquor; if you can sleep without the aid of drugs; if you can honestly say that deep in your heart you have no prejudice against creed or color, religion or politics; then you my friend, your almost as good as your dog." This poem is dedicated to two kinds of people: 1) Animal lovers, and 2) Those who can ***Stop, Listen, Absorb, & Act*** *"Be alert and of sober mind, love each other deeply, and use your gifts to serve others." 1 Peter 4 :1-2*

The Art of an Apology

If your actions have caused hurt feelings, anger, or deep-seated ill will, an apology is in order. Apologizing is not an acknowledgement of weakness. A *sincere* apology can have a tremendous amount of healing power for both the receiver and the giver

The RRR's - An effective apology will communicate the three R's: **Regret, Responsibility,** and **Remedy**

- *Regret:* Communicate the regret you feel sincerely.
  - Even in cases where your intention was not to upset or hurt someone, the apology must come from your heart.

- *Responsibility:* Do not make excuses or blame others. Accept total responsibility for your actions.
  - Don't say, "I'm sorry about what happened, but you shouldn't have..."

- *Remedy:* A meaningful apology should include a commitment to not repeat the behavior
  - It might also include an offer of restitution.

Tools
4 Life

Unwrapping Your "Presence"

The greatest gift we can give does not come in a box. It comes from our heart. "Love is slow to suspect but quick to trust; slow to condemn but quick to justify; slow to offend but quick to defend; slow to expose but quick to shield; slow to reprimand but quick to empathize; slow to belittle but quick to appreciate; slow to demand but quick to give; slow to provoke but quick to help; slow to resent but quick to forgive." (TWFYT) The scriptures give great guidelines on how to turn a holiday season into a lifestyle of learning to love.

- Love believes all things - love teaches me to look beyond the hurt that I am in with someone I care about
- Love brings hope - love teaches me to see the potential in people and not the mud they are stuck in
- Love endures – love teaches me to throw an anchor into stormy waters (1Corinthians 13)

Tools
4 Life

Wait, Change is coming

Are you waiting to find a solution to a problem? Are you struggling because things aren't falling into place for the change you desire? Have you noticed that when you get what you want you are waiting for something else? Have you ever said, "I can't wait for this to be over!"? The fact is, we live in me-itus world where we eat when we're hungry, we buy something we think we need, we chase things that aren't good for us and we make quick decisions that ripple into other decisions, which eventually snowball into a rock at the bottom of a hill. This fast-paced "give me what I want" society is ambushing the things God has in store for you. We are being bred and conditioned with a drive-through mentality to not wait for anything. Consider the long process of a butterfly evolving from its cocoon. If we try to rush God's purpose and process, we can produce something that is deformed and can't get off the ground to fly. Job said, "All the days of my life I will wait till my change comes." Job 14:14 We've heard it said, "Good things come to those who wait." The real question is: WHO are you waiting for? What God has for you is worth more than any season of waiting or any price you must pay. He won't disappoint you. Wait, change is coming.

Tools
4 Life

What Voice Drives Me

There are 2 voices that are competing for your ears. Both have different roots and both have different results. One voice is rooted in anger, pain, and jealousy. It is screaming injustice and recruiting people to stand and fight; to roam, kill, and destroy. These voices are getting louder and harder to shut out as crowds and armies are forming in our streets and along our borders. The result of this voice is death. The other is a "small still voice" that is rooted in love, peace, and mercy. It is the voice of God through His Word that is calling us to seek Him and His righteousness. When we hear and respond to this voice, the result is a peace that surpasses all understanding and a life beyond what we see. The loud voice is recruiting those who are filled with rage, while the small still voice is recruiting those who are filled with a hunger to know God. The choice is ours and it depends on the desire for vengeance or the desire for mercy; determining end the result, life or death. "As for me and my house we will serve the Lord" Joshua 24:15

Tools
4 Life

You Are Not Alone

Have you ever been so overwhelmed and thought the odds against me don't look good? I am being schooled by an incredible woman who is facing the most horrific death sentence of multiple diseases that I have ever witnessed. She is Jesus with skin as her strength to love and release her husband and others in their suffering for her is a witness of God's love. All through scripture God's love multiplies Himself for us to fight as He gives us victory through the cross. *"For I am convinced that nothing can ever separate us from his love. Death can't, and life can't. The angels won't, and all the powers of hell itself cannot keep God's love away. Our fears for today, our worries about tomorrow, or where we are—high above the sky, or in the deepest ocean—nothing will ever be able to separate us from the love of God demonstrated by our Lord Jesus Christ when he died for us. Romans 8:38-39* I want to thank my friend for teaching the power of LOVE over death. You are a true witness that "You Are Not Alone".

Tools
4 Life

Attitudes Change the Course of life

Attitude is one of the first things people see in making an assumption. Here is the best attitude quote I have ever read. "The longer I live, the more I realize the impact of attitude on life. Attitude, to me, is more important than facts. It is more important than the past, than education, than money, than circumstances, than failures, than successes, than what other people think or say or do. It is more important than appearance, giftedness or skill. It will make or break a company...a church...a home. The remarkable thing is we have a choice every day regarding the attitude we will embrace for that day. We cannot change our past...we cannot change the fact that people will act in a certain way. We cannot change the inevitable. The only thing we can do is play on the one string we have, and that is our attitude...I am convinced that life is 10% what happens to me and 90% how I react to it. And so it is with you...we are in charge of our attitudes."— Charles R. Swindoll

A Touch in the Darkest Hour

Every one of us will personally experience and/or know someone who is/has been in their darkest hour. This is the place where there is no light at the end of the tunnel. We lost someone recently (Robin Williams) who suffered in his darkest hour. Man, has labeled a multitude of mental health disorders that have a root in depression. Labels validate one's pain and give them a reason to sink lower in the name of their diagnosis. Pharmaceutical companies are gaining millions from varied prescriptions in attempts to bring comfort in the darkest hour. The critical thing that must take place for survival is to remove the label of victim, replaced with a label of victor. The scriptures talk of resources from heaven in the midst of a paralyzed state of mind. When Peter was facing his darkest hour, on the eve of his execution, "the church was earnestly praying." Prayer behind the scenes is a source of unknown spiritual strength. Twice, when Jesus was in His darkest hour, an Angel touched Him and gave Him strength to move forward in his immobile state. The scriptures are full of times when angels provide strength when the tunnel is dark. When we get our senses and strength back, our faith in Christ allows us to live and move forward. Whether we are in our earthly body suit or heavenly body suit, we live in eternity through Christ.

Tools
4 Life

Big Ears are better than a Big Mouth

Have you ever wondered why we have 2 ears and 1 mouth? We might be born with the ability to hear, but we must learn how to listen. If we increase our intake and decrease our output we can learn when, where, and how to be effective listeners. Effective listening is not easy. It takes concentration and energy. The following are a few hints to help us become active listeners.

- Respect: regard the speaker as worthy of your attention
- Stay focused on what is being said: it is so easy to mind wander and not be present
- Ask questions: this allows clarification for both the sender and the receiver
- Give feedback: paraphrasing in your own words reassures understanding

Tools
4 Life

Don't Give Up Your Dream, Revise Your Plan

Have you ever had the wind blown out of your sails in regards to your career or your calling? Sometimes we need to step back and approach things differently. General S. Patton Jr said "Successful generals make plans to fit the circumstances, but do not try to create circumstances to fit plans." When we are so focused and locked onto a clear plan to reach our potential and destination, we can close the door for other opportunities. Our inflexibility can cause us to stick to "the plan" no matter what and derail us from the end result. Sometimes it is best and wiser to explore other options to get to the finish line. Don't give up on your dream, revise your plan. "The question that faces the strategic decision maker is not what his/her organization should do tomorrow. It is: What do we have to do today to be ready for an uncertain tomorrow?" (Peter Ducker) There are certain things we can do that can help us face the challenges and uncertainties of tomorrow; 1) Put your faith in God. King David wrote, "The steps of a good man are ordered by the Lord." There is an anchored Divine Peace when we let God be in charge. 2) Learn to be flexible. Flexibility opens windows that appear to be closed. 3) Learn to adapt. "The only way to make sense out of change is to plunge into it, move with it, and join the dance." Alan W. Watts

Tools
4 Life

It's OK to Be Different

Have you wondered why it is so easy to talk to some people and so difficult to talk to others? Have you ever caught yourself wanting to disappear from a room when someone pushes your exit button? It is so important for us to realize that people have different communication styles that might rub us the wrong way. Once I accept that not everyone is like me, my world gets a little bigger. Here are some different communication styles.

- LEAVE ME ALONE style; usually quiet, alone and introverted
- TAKE CHARGE style: frank, assertive, and controlling
- YOU MAKE THE CHOICE style: non-attention seeking, patient, and passive
- IT'S ALL ABOUT ME style: likes the lime light, spontaneous, and persuasive

Tools
4 Life

A Year of Significance

I recently witnessed a sunrise while flying above storm clouds hovering the land below. I realized then that God had bigger plans for me that were above the circumstances of life. With the New Year here most of us desire to make this a significant year. The best way we can do that is to be drawn, driven, directed, and dedicated to the path that is laid out for us. *"Along unfamiliar paths I will guide them; I will turn the darkness into light before them and make the rough places smooth. These are the things I will do; I will not forsake them." Isaiah 42:16.* I must be **drawn;** "Draw near to God and He will draw near to me" James 4:8, **driven;** *16 We never give up. Our bodies are gradually dying, but we ourselves are being made stronger each day." 2 Corinthians 4:16,* **directed;** *"Your word is a lamp for my feet, a light on my path" Psalm 119:105,* and **dedicated;** *"And whatever you do or say, do it as a representative of the Lord Jesus, giving thanks through him to God the Father." Colossians 3:17.* Let's make this a year of significance and accomplish great things. *"The LORD will work out his plans for my life—for your faithful love, O LORD, endures forever." Psalm 138:8*

Tools
4 Life

Friendship Roles

Studies have shown that an average person can have up to 400 friendships over a lifetime. We have friends that do a lot more for us than we do for them. We have friends that are fun to be around but can be flaky and leave us hanging. We have friends that are awesome but gone before we know it. We have friends that make everything happen for us whether we want it or not. We have friends that will give us a shoulder to cry on and then use ours to do the same. We have friends who have been with us in our rebellious times. We have friends that started out bright and burned up in a flame. We have friends that we can tell stories about as they have helped shape us. We have friends that we outgrow. We have some friends (like family) that we are stuck with. If you are like me, the **CLOSE** friends are very few. A new study suggests Americans' lists of the **CLOSE** type has shrunk to two, down from three confidantes in a study 25 years ago. These are the few friends that put air under your wings and bring life to your bones. If you are anything like me, these friends are on sacred ground and held close in our innermost court. I thank God for my very special friends and I thank God for the 400 friendships that have helped me in my journey. Be grateful and let your friends know how much you appreciate them.

Tools
4 Life

Cutting the Anchors of Guilt and Shame

Being ashamed of who we are or guilty of what we have done or what has been done to us are two anchors in life that immobilize us and keep us from moving forward. Even when we think we have succeeded in hiding our feelings, thoughts, and attitudes our guilt and shame comes out in other ways. Some of these behaviors can include compulsive behaviors, sexual addictions, overeating, chemical and alcohol abuse, and depression. Here are a few tools to help you get rid of the guilt and shame.

Stop beating yourself up. You are not a whack-a-mole

Treat yourself to fun and innovative things

Open up to fresh thinking and get rid of the negative self-talk

Power for the future by releasing the power of the anchor

Tools
4 Life

The Roller Coaster of Loss

I've heard it said that when you lose a parent you lose your history, when you lose a spouse or sibling you lose your present, and when you lose a child you lose your future. The pain of losing someone you love or care deeply about is extremely difficult to navigate. I often think of the grieving process as a roller coaster. The grind of the uphill climb takes you up and over into an uncontrollable decent downward. Then comes the whip-lashing curves that toss you from side to side only to make the grinding climb again. Each day is filled with the emotions of climbing and falling with all the twists and turns of surviving one day at a time. The only thing that keeps us from falling all the way out is a seat belt and safety bar. The seat-belt and safety bar must be fastened and secured for us to survive. The fiber of the seat-belt and the composition of the bar that holds us together is made up of the things that we can't see because the things we see will fade away but the things we can't see will last forever. That's why we never give up. Allow faith to begin to fill the empty cave of your being. Hold onto its handle bar and fasten its belt around your waist as you begin the uphill grind of facing the roller coaster one second, one minute, one hour, and one day at a time.

Tools
4 Life

The Empty Chair

A daughter asked a pastor to pray with her dad. When he arrived, he found Joe lying in bed, head propped up on two pillows, and an empty chair beside his bed. "I guess you were expecting me," he said. "No, who are you?" "Your daughter called me and when I saw the empty chair, I figured you were expecting me." "The empty chair", said the dad. "I've never told anyone this, not even my daughter. All of my life I have never known how to pray. I used to hear about prayer, but it always went right over my head. Four years ago my best friend said to me, "Joe, prayer is a simple matter of having a conversation with Jesus. Here's what I suggest. Sit down on a chair, place an empty chair in front of you, and in faith see Jesus on the chair. It's not spooky because he promised, "I'll be with you always." Then just speak to Him and listen in the same way you're doing with me right now." "So, I tried it and liked it so much that I do it a couple of hours every day. I'm careful, though. If my daughter saw me talking to an empty chair, she'd either have a nervous breakdown or send me off to the funny farm." Deeply moved, the pastor prayed and left. Two nights later the daughter called the pastor with the news of her dad's passing. "When I left the house, he called me over to his bedside, told me one of his corny jokes, and kissed me on the cheek. When I got back from the store an hour later, I found him dead. But there was something strange, In fact, beyond strange--kind of weird. Apparently, just before Daddy died, he leaned over and rested his head on a chair beside the bed."

The True Candy of Life

A man observed a sad and rugged looking kid staring into the candy store window. He took him inside and told the cashier to give him a bag and fill it with whatever he wanted. The little guys eyes got so big and he began to fill his mouth with the incredible sugary delights. As the bag was filled and the cheeks of the young boy were bulging from the side, the man asked the lad if he could have some. The boy's joy suddenly turned into fear as he grabbed the bag, held it tight, and went running out of the store screaming, "Mine Mine!!" Sometimes in life we take for granted the heart, intention, and hand of life around us. When we hold on to things we become selfish and ungrateful and miss the opportunity to receive and give. The best antidote for a selfish heart is a giving heart. True happiness doesn't come from filling our bag at the candy store. Happiness comes from helping to fill others bags with the sweet things in life. We are not supposed to be a storehouse. We're supposed to be an outlet. We are created to be a blessing to others around us. Let's look at every opportunity to fill others bags with the true candy of life.

Tools
4 Life

Three Rules of Life

I have had the honor of being a husband, dad, coach, instructor, pastor, counselor, and friend. Lou Holtz, former Notre Dame Football coach, has motivated myself and thousands of students and athletes with three rules of life; 1) Give everything you have to the best of your ability, 2) Do the right thing, and 3) Show people you care. These three principles can be applied to every person as we navigate through the daily race that each of us run. When applied, these rules will take the average person and give him/her the ability to succeed and be fulfilled at their highest level. 1) Put everything you got on the field and play *through the whistle.* Whether at work, home, or play, give it your all emotionally, physically and spiritually. 2) The average person makes 35,000 choices a day. Many of these choices piggy back on the previous one. If we can purposefully do the right thing, good things will follow. 3) People around us will respond positively and favorably if they know they are cared for. When we go out of our way to benefit someone else, the rewards are intrinsic. These three rules will allow us to push through our day from the inside out. The speedbumps that we face during the day may slow us down but we will keep moving.

Tools
4 Life

What's in My Bucket?

The book How *Full Is Your Bucket* provides a great picture of the interactions of relationships. Every one of us has a bucket and ladle. We are at our best when the bucket is full and overflowing. We are at our worst when our bucket is empty. Our ladle can either pour into someone else's bucket filling it or dip into and emptying it. Whenever we fill someone else's bucket we in turn fill our own. If we choose to talk negatively about someone we drain them and our self. If we choose to say something positive, we fill their bucket and ours. Whatever is in my bucket is what I give. If my bucket is full of anger and/or fear, my relationships are going to be splashed with anger and/or fear. If my bucket is full of love, my relationships will be soaked with love. So, the question we need to ask ourselves is what's in my bucket? God is love, so ask God to fill your bucket with His living water and scoop out to others whenever you get the chance.

Tools
4 Life

Preparing For Battle

The war is on. It is a battle for the minds, hearts, and hands of people - between the forces of good and evil, between God and Satan. The male species of the Alaskan Bull Moose battle for dominance during the fall breeding season, literally going head-to-head with antlers crunching together as they collide. Often the antlers, their only weapon, are broken. The heftiest moose, with the largest and strongest antlers, triumphs. Therefore, the battle fought in the fall is really won during the summer, when the moose eat continually. The one that consumes the best diet for growing antlers and gaining weight will be the heavyweight in the fight. Those that eat inadequately have weaker antlers and less bulk. Spiritual battles await as Satan roams and seeks to destroy. Will we be victorious, or will we fall? So much depends on what we do now. The bull-moose principle: Enduring faith, strength, and wisdom for trials are best developed before they're needed. We don't fight for the victory; we fight from the victory that Jesus gave us. The next few weeks I will be covering the spiritual armor that is necessary to walk in victory.

Stepping into a New Season

Life is full of change, just as the four seasons that are based on the rotation of the earth as it orbits the sun. The temperature of our personal seasons can be as cold as the winter while we experience the separation of warmth from family and friends. This could be a time when the night time seems as if it will never end; the long nights when the tears seem like they will never stop flowing. The morning comes, the tears cease, and the joy returns to your spirit as a new season brings springtime weather and the budding of new life, hope, and purpose. Summer season comes with the heat that helps circulate our being and we see the fruit of our labor and love. Then comes the fall season where everything becomes dormant and either dies or goes into seclusion and hibernation for the winter. Our lives will change, and we will enter and exit many seasons. God doesn't measure seasons with clocks and calendars, but through truth and revelation. Every season we go through has purpose in maturing and completing us. There are some things to know and learn about seasons as we step in and out of them. They bring new **changes**, new **challenges**, and new **champions**. We are all either entering a season, in the middle of a season, or coming out of a season. Keep stepping and you will become a weathered champion.

Tools
4 Life

The Power of Sandpaper

Sandpaper has a purpose to smooth out roughness. The grain used depends on the surface that needs to be sanded and smoothed. ***The greatest reward from a relationship is not what we get out of it but what we become through it.*** If we can focus on conflict as a chance to grow rather than the pain and bleeding from the process we can become mature and complete through it. The struggles we have in life make our surface very rough. The relationships we have not only sand our edges us out but they allow us to be smooth for others to come near to. Here are a few things to think about.

- View conflict as positive sandpaper
- The rougher it is the more I can learn
- Go through the process of sanding knowing that the end result is better

Tools
4 Life

When Change is in the Air

What should I do when change is inevitable? Sometimes we see it coming and other times we get blindsided. Change is never easy. Let's look at a few tools to use when we are faced with a fork in the road. **CHOOSE HAPPINESS** – What we choose to focus on largely determines our level of happiness. Our thoughts control our actions which determine our results. Instead of seeing change as the end of something, see it as the beginning of something new. If we can mentally reframe things that make us unhappy into something that makes us happy we can learn to skip rather than fall. **STAY POSITIVE** – Positive thoughts pave the road for positive attitudes and effective relationships. One of the first casualties of change that we view as negative is our relationships. Staying positive ads mortar between the bricks. We have a choice to swim in one of two pools, positive or negative. Either pool will soak you. **KEEP AN OPEN MIND** - Too often we try to manage a direction where we think things are going and we forget that God is in control. If I can expose myself to information and experiences beyond what I know I will mature and become more complete. One of the most powerful tools we can ever use in life is flexibility. It opens doors that appear to be locked tight. In the words of Jesus ""*Let not your hearts be troubled. Believe in God; believe also in me. John 14:1*

Tools
4 Life

Overcoming the Past

It's impossible to succeed in life without overcoming the past. We spend far too much time and energy on things we can't change rather than on the most important thing we can change – our attitude. Life is like an automobile that can spin off the road. We must get out of the ditch and keep moving forward. Here are some important things to do to get back on the road.

- Get back in the driver's seat
- Keep looking through the front windshield
- Use the rear-view mirror to remind you where you came from
- Know where you came from because it is paving the way for where you are going
- Most important: keep your foot on the gas or you won't go anywhere

Tools
4 Life

Test Your Feelings

Feelings are a wonderful thing but not always trustworthy. They can give us insights into new and exciting situations. They can flutter with anticipation and allow our blood to reach the ends of capillaries we never knew existed. They can fill our mind and heart with passion and direction. Our feelings allow us to draw closer to each other and God. The reality is that feelings are subjective. We can't always trust them. An event or situation can trigger a reaction to old feelings. Sometimes when old feelings creep back in we feel fearful, ashamed, unloved, hopeless, angry, inadequate, helpless, resentful, bitter, victimized, and vengeful. I know this list can go on and on. A bad ending to a relationship, conflict on the job or at home, change, stress from a traumatic event, or disease and sickness can all ignite our feelings. Sometimes these feelings can come out of nowhere at any time. We could have disastrous results if we relied solely on the things we feel, see, and hear. We are not defined by our feelings. We are defined by our head, heart, and hands all being aligned together. Always test your feelings before reacting. Allow yourself to be cautionary with your past experiences and the counsel of those you trust.

Tools
4 Life

The Antidote for Complaining

Complaining is like a virus. It gets into our system and goes through us like a disease. It takes the joy out of our spirit, turns peace into chaos, turns positivity into negativity, turns success into failure, and changes good relationships to bad ones. The best antidote for complaining is to be grateful. A grateful attitude changes perception and reality.

G – Grateful - Being grateful and negative is like mixing oil and water. It is impossible to be grateful and negative at the same time.

R – Release – When we complain we hold onto and squeeze whatever it is that is bothering us. Releasing loosens the grip of complaining and allows us to be open to collecting new information.

A – Align - Being grateful realigns us with positive things.

T – Think – Being grateful allows us to think about things that are positive and good.

E – Encourage – Instead of complaining about what people have done wrong, focus on what they have done right.

F – Flight – Being grateful allows us to run away from the things that grip us.

U – Understanding – Being grateful brings an awareness and understanding to things we could complain about.

L – Learn - Being grateful gives us the ability to learn from the good and the bad

Tools
4 Life

Your Story Matters

Every one of us has a story. Some are big and some are small. Our big stories are made up of our culture, gender, personalities, belongings, skills, beliefs, victories, losses, and desires. All of these reveal the direction of our lives and help make up the big picture of who we are. They are like cinder blocks. The small stories are the mortar and substance that fill in the gaps of the big stories. The little stories are the connecting points. They are the glue that pulls everything together. These are the everyday happenings that slip by almost unnoticed. It is the little stories that shape us and mold us. A few of the things that make up our small stories are our attitudes, emotions, fears, thoughts, perceptions, and actions. Our core values are the foundation for our stories both big and small. The important thing to hold tight to is that your story matters.

I hope the pages of this book have encouraged you and given you some insight and tools on your journey. *GPS: Your Guide through Personal Storms* can be used throughout your lifetime. Please share with others, as we all need one another.

Future Books Soon to Be Released by Dr. James Coyle

Tools 4 Life: Daily Inspirational Guide
Your Story Matters: Life-Changing Stories

Works Cited

"Lessons from Alaska and Bad Weather to Help Building Your Oil Pipeline," Sean Glaze, Great Results Team Building, http://greatresultsteambuilding.net/lessons-alaska-bad-weather-help-building-oil-pipeline/.

"35,000 Decisions: The Great Choices of Strategic Leaders," Joel Hoomans, Roberts Wesleyan College, March 20, 2015. Web, August 9, 2016. http://go.roberts.edu/leadingedge/the-great-choices-of-strategic-leaders.

Peterson, Eugene H. *The Message: The Bible in Contemporary Language.* Colorado Springs: NAVPress, 2005.

Rath, Tom, and Donald O. Clifton. *How Full Is Your Bucket?: Positive Strategies for Work and Life.* New York: Gallup, 2004.

"Shake It Off," United Christian Broadcasters, December 29, 2012. Web, August 1, 2016. http://www.ucb.co.uk/print/print/word-for-today-13170.html.